STICKER ENCYCLOPEDIA

TOTAL TRACTOR

About this book

HOW TO USE THIS BOOK

Read the information pages, and then search for the relevant stickers in the back of the book to fill in the gaps. Use the sticker outlines and labels to help you.

There are lots of extra stickers that you can use to decorate the scenes in the back of the book. It's up to you where you put them all. The most important thing is to have lots of sticker fun!

DK | Penguin Random House

Author and Consultant Josephine Roberts

Senior Editor Jolyon Goddard
Project Editors Manisha Majithia, Radhika Haswani
Editor Shambhavi Thatte
Senior Designers Ann Cannings, Nidhi Mehra
Project Designer Jaileen Kaur
US Senior Editor Shannon Beatty
US Editor Elizabeth Searcy
Managing Editors Laura Gilbert, Alka Thakur Hazarika
Managing Art Editors Diane Peyton Jones, Romi Chakraborty
DTP Designers Nityanand Kumar, Sachin Gupta
Picture Researcher Rituraj Singh
Jacket Coordinator Issy Walsh
Jacket Designers Sonny Flynn, Kartik Gera
Jacket Editor Radhika Haswani
Preproduction Producer Sophie Chatellier
Producer Basia Ossowska
Delhi Team Head Malavika Talukder
Creative Director Helen Senior
Publishing Director Sarah Larter

First American Edition, 2019
Published in the United States by DK Publishing
1450 Broadway, Suite 801, New York, NY 10018

Copyright © 2019 Dorling Kindersley Limited
DK, a Division of Penguin Random House LLC
19 20 21 22 23 10 9 8 7 6 5 4 3 2 1
001–316111–Oct/2019

All rights reserved.
Without limiting the rights under the copyright reserved above, no part of this publication may be reproduced, stored in or introduced into a retrieval system, or transmitted, in any form, or by any means (electronic, mechanical, photocopying, recording, or otherwise), without the prior written permission of the copyright owner.
Published in Great Britain by Dorling Kindersley Limited.

A catalog record for this book is available from the Library of Congress.
ISBN: 978-1-4654-8894-7

DK books are available at special discounts when purchased in bulk for sales promotions, premiums, fund-raising, or educational use. For details, contact: DK Publishing Special Markets, 1450 Broadway, Suite 801, New York, NY 10018
SpecialSales@dk.com

Printed and bound in China

A WORLD OF IDEAS:
SEE ALL THERE IS TO KNOW

www.dk.com

DK would like to thank Marie Greenwood for editorial assistance, Lucy Sims for design assistance, and Kathleen Teece for proofreading.

The publisher would like to thank the following for their kind permission to reproduce their photographs:
(Key: a-above; b-below/bottom; c-center; f-far; l-left; r-right; t-top; row:column on pages 66, 67, 70, 71)

1 Alamy Stock Photo: Taina Sohlman (crb). **Dorling Kindersley**: Peter Goddard (cl). **Getty Images**: Bloomberg (clb). **2 Alamy Stock Photo**: Joerg Huettenhoelscher (cla). **3 Dorling Kindersley**: David Bowman (crb); Doubleday Swineshead Depot. (clb). Versatile: (b). **4–5 Dorling Kindersley**: Chandlers Ltd. **5 Dorling Kindersley**: Doubleday Swineshead Depot (crb). **6 Dorling Kindersley**: Paul Rackham (bl). **6–7 Dreamstime.com**: Petr Švec. **7 Dreamstime.com**: 1000words (crb). **8 Dorling Kindersley**: Paul Rackham (b). **9 Dorling Kindersley**: Paul Rackham (b). **10 Dreamstime.com**: Marco Saracco. **Fotolia**: Olena Pantiukh (cra). **11 Alamy Stock Photo**: William Arthur (b). **12–13 Dorling Kindersley**: Rabtrak (cb). **Dreamstime.com**: Lane Erickson. **14 Alamy Stock Photo**: Arco Images GmbH (b). **15 J.C. Bamford Excavators Ltd**: (b). **16 Dreamstime.com**: Palex66. **17 Dorling Kindersley**: Lister Wilder (br). **18 Dorling Kindersley**: Doubleday Swineshead Depot (cl). **18–19 Dorling Kindersley**: Paul Rackham (bc). **19 Dorling Kindersley**: Peter Goddard (cra). **20–21 Dreamstime.com**: Colicaranica. **20 Dorling Kindersley**: Chandlers Ltd (b). **22 Dreamstime.com**: Maksudkr (cla). **iStockphoto.com**: VR_Studio (cra). **22–23 iStockphoto.com**: AVTG (b). **23 Alamy Stock Photo**: Andia (cla). **Dreamstime.com**: Saša Prudkov (cra). **24–25 Dreamstime.com**: Ifeelstock. **25 Getty Images**: Education Images / Universal Images Group (tr). **26–27 Dreamstime.com**: Taweepat Larpparisut; Anton Petrychenko (ca). **27 Dreamstime.com**: Vladimir Melnik (tc). Versatile: (br). **28 Dreamstime.com**: Jon Helgason (br/Helmet); Alexander Levchenko (br). **28–29 Dreamstime.com**: Mrtwister. **30 Alamy Stock Photo**: bronstein (bl). **30–31 Dreamstime.com**: Artem Kolomeichuk. **32–33 123RF.com**: Ryan Carter (bc). **Dreamstime.com**: Taweepat Larpparisut. **33 Alamy Stock Photo**: Alvey & Towers Picture Library (crb). **34–35 Dreamstime.com**: Gkuna. **36–37 iStockphoto.com**: Piotr Wytrazek. **38–39 Dreamstime.com**: Marko Sarenac. **40 Alamy Stock Photo**: imageBROKER (cra); David Robertson (clb); Simon Perkin (crb). **42 Massey Ferguson - AGCO Ltd.**: (tl). **Alamy Stock Photo**: FLPA (cr/John Deere 9400). **Dorling Kindersley**: Chandlers Ltd (Massey Ferguson MF 7618 Tractor Parts, c); James River Equipment (tc); Paul Rackham (cr, cl); Roger and Fran Desborough (crb); Robin Simons (br/John Deere Unstyled). **Dreamstime.com**: Bluetoes67 (bc/John Deere tractor); Mohammed Anwarul Kabir Choudhury (cb). **Fotolia**: Olena Pantiukh (bc/Hen). **Getty Images**: Bloomberg (ca); Science & Society Picture Library (br). J.C. Bamford Excavators Ltd: (bl). **43 Dorling Kindersley**: Henry Flashman (tc); Paul Rackham (cra/Cletrac General, cla, crb, c, cb/Waterloo Boy Model N, 1920, cb, cb/Lanz Bulldog D2206, ca, clb, br, bc, bc/MOM Fordson Model F); Robin Simons (cl); Peter Goddard (cra); Lister Wilder (tr/Crawler). **Dreamstime.com**: 1000words (tr); Saša Prudkov (cr). **Getty Images**: Science & Society Picture Library (tl). **J.C. Bamford Excavators Ltd**: (bl). **46 Alamy Stock Photo**: Andia (bc); MediaWorldImages (ca/Ferguson 35X); Arco Images GmbH (cra/Fendt Vario 939); William Arthur (tr). **Dorling Kindersley**: Chandlers Ltd (cra, ca/Kubota L3200, crb); Paul Rackham (tl, ca/Ford 9N, clb/Lanz Bulldog D2206); J Hardstaff (tc); James River Equipment (cb/aJohn Deere 160D LC); Doubleday Holbeach Depot (bl, br); Henry Flashman (ca); John Bowen-Jones (cla); Peter Goddard (crb/Allis Chalmers). **Dreamstime.com**: 1000words (crb/Horse Plough); Bluetoes67 (clb); Jon Helgason (c). **Getty Images**: Bloomberg (cb). **47 Alamy Stock Photo**: Andia (cb); William Arthur (tl, tc, tc/Exhaust); bronstein (cra/Unimog U400). **Dorling Kindersley**: Chandlers Ltd (br, ca); Doubleday Swineshead Depot (cb/John Deere 6210R); Lister Wilder (cr/Crawler, crb); James River Equipment (cla, cl); Keystone Tractor Works (bc); Paul Rackham (bl, tl/Hart-Parr 18-36, c); Daniel Ward (clb); Peter Goddard (crb/Allis Chalmers). **Dreamstime.com**: Alexander Levchenko (clb/Cement); Photobac (br/Yellow bulldozer). **New Holland Agriculture**: (tr, crb/kps_3620). **50 Alamy Stock Photo**: Andia (ca); FLPA (tl); John Gaffen 2 (tr/Talus MB-H Crawler); William Arthur (crb); dpa picture alliance (clb); Taina Sohlman (br). **Dorling Kindersley**: Mick Browning, Tanks, Trucks and Firepower Show (cra/armoured carrier); James River Equipment (tc, crb/John Deere 650K, tc/excavator); Keystone Tractor Works (bc); Paul Rackham (tr, cla). **Dreamstime.com**: Saša Prudkov (bl). **Fotolia**: Olena Pantiukh (cb/hen). **iStockphoto.com**: VR_Studio (c). J.C. Bamford Excavators Ltd: (cb, cr, cra, cra/FST_4000_06). New Holland Agriculture: (cb/kps_3620). 51 Massey Ferguson - AGCO Ltd.: (clb). **Alamy Stock Photo**: Arco Images GmbH (tl); John Gaffen 2 (cl). **Dorling Kindersley**: Chandlers Ltd (cb/Cat TH406); Doubleday Swineshead Depot. (br); James River Equipment (cb/John Deere 333E); Paul Rackham (ca, crb/Ford 9N, cr, tc/MOM Fordson, tr/Hart-Parr 18-36); Miller Mining / Mike Dunning (cra); Roger and Fran Desborough (c); Peter Goddard (c/wheel); Doubleday Swineshead Depot (ca/Harvester). **Dreamstime.com**: Bluetoes67 (bl, tr/Harvester); Maksudkr (tc). **Fotolia**: Olena Pantiukh (tr/hen, cb/hen). **J.C. Bamford Excavators Ltd**: (crb). **New Holland Agriculture**: (tr/Braud_9090X). **54 Alamy Stock Photo**: Arco Images GmbH (ca); picturesbyrob (cla); FLPA (clb); John Gaffen 2 (clb/MB-H Crawler); Robert Shantz (br); Joerg Huettenhoelscher (tr). **Dorling Kindersley**: Doubleday Swineshead Depot (tl); James River Equipment (cb, bc); Doubleday Holbeach Depot (ca/Xerion 3800, cb/Puma 230 CVX); Henry Flashman (ca/Minneapolis-Moline UDLX). **Dreamstime.com**: Bluetoes67 (ca/6215r tractor); Saša Prudkov (clb/harvester); Alexander Levchenko (clb/Cement). **Versatile**: (cra). **55 Fendt International - AGCO GmbH**: (cl/Fertig). **Alamy Stock Photo**: Alvey & Towers Picture Library (br); Simon Perkin (ca); FLPA (cr); bronstein (tl). **Dorling Kindersley**: Mick Browning, Tanks, Trucks and Firepower Show (clb); J Hardstaff (cra); Grimme UK (tc); Paul Rackham (clb/Waterloo Boy Model N, cla, c, tl/Hart-Parr 18-36); Lister Wilder (cb, cra/Tractor); James River Equipment (crb, cb/843K). **Dreamstime.com**: Bluetoes67 (cl). John Deere Walldorf GmbH & Co. KG: (tr). **58 Massey Ferguson - AGCO Ltd**: (tl/Hill climber). **Alamy Stock Photo**: Arco Images GmbH (tr/Fendt Vario 939); David Robertson (clb); imageBROKER (cb); Hayden Richard Verry (cra); John Gaffen 2 (bl/MB-H Crawler). **Dorling Kindersley**: David Bowman (br); Mick Browning, Tanks, Trucks and Firepower Show (cr); Paul Rackham (clb/Lanz Bulldog D2206, crb/Caterpillar D7); James River Equipment (clb/SV400, cra/SV400, ca); Chandlers Ltd (cra/Kubota L3200, tl); Peter Goddard (bl). **Dreamstime.com**: Bluetoes67 (tr); Mohammed Anwarul Kabir Choudhury (cb/Potash); Jon Helgason (cra/Helmet). **Fotolia**: Olena Pantiukh (cra/hen, crb/hen). **Getty Images**: Science & Society Picture Library (cl, crb). New Holland Agriculture: (tc, crb/T9.505, cla, ca/Braud_9090X). **59 AGCO Ltd**: (tl/MT965C). **Massey Ferguson - AGCO Ltd**: (bl). **Alamy Stock Photo**: bronstein (cra/Unimog U400, tc/Unimog U400). ©2019 CNH Industrial America LLC. All rights reserved. Case IH is a trademark registered in the United States and many other countries, owned by or licensed to CNH Industrial N.V., its subsidiaries or affiliates.: (tr). **Dorling Kindersley**: James River Equipment (br, cl, clb); Paul Rackham (tl, tc/Ford 9N, ca/Ford 9N, cra/Cletrac General, crb/Hart-Parr 18-36); Lister Wilder (c); Robin Simons (ca/JD Unstyled B). **Dreamstime.com**: 1000words (cr); Saša Prudkov (tc); Bluetoes67 (cb); Mohammed Anwarul Kabir Choudhury (ca/Potash); Jon Helgason (c/Helmet). **Getty Images**: Bloomberg (cra). John Deere Walldorf GmbH & Co. KG: (clb/9620RX). **Max Holder GmbH Mahdenstr**: (crb). **New Holland Agriculture**: (cla). **62 Alamy Stock Photo**: Andia (crb); picturesbyrob (clb). **Dorling Kindersley**: Doubleday Swineshead Depot (tr); Miller Mining / Mike Dunning (br); James River Equipment (cla, cr); Lister Wilder (cra, tl). **Dreamstime.com**: Mohammed Anwarul Kabir Choudhury (cla/Potash). **Fotolia**: Olena Pantiukh (cr/hen). **J.C. Bamford Excavators Ltd**: (c). **63 123RF.com**: Anton Starikov (br); tomwang / Wang Tom (cra). **Alamy Stock Photo**: Robert Shantz (bl). **Dorling Kindersley**: Doubleday Swineshead Depot. (tl); Lister Wilder (cla); Doubleday Swineshead Depot (tr). **Dreamstime.com**: Jon Helgason (cb). **iStockphoto.com**: MilaSCH (cl). **66 123RF.com**: Anton Starikov (cra). **Alamy Stock Photo**: Andia (3:2); FLPA (1:8); John Gaffen 2 (3:8); bronstein (2:7). **Dorling Kindersley**: Mick Browning, Tanks, Trucks and Firepower Show (2:9); Keystone Tractor Works (3:5); Paul Rackham (2:6, 1:4); Miller Mining / Mike Dunning (cla); Doubleday Swineshead Depot (tl); Henry Flashman (1:1); Chandlers Ltd (3:4); James River Equipment (2:2, 1:7); Peter Goddard (2:1). **Dreamstime.com**: Mohammed Anwarul Kabir Choudhury (clb); Hansenn (cr); Anton Petrychenko (tr); Jon Helgason (cb/Helmet). **Fotolia**: Olena Pantiukh (crb). **J.C. Bamford Excavators Ltd**: (cl, 3:9, cb). **New Holland Agriculture**: (1:3). **67 123RF.com**: isselee / Eric Isselee (cr). **Massey Ferguson - AGCO Ltd**: (tr). **Alamy Stock Photo**: FLPA (2:8); imageBROKER (cra); Zoonar GmbH (tl). **Dorling Kindersley**: David Bowman (cb); Paul Rackham (2:1, 2:4); Lister Wilder (2:3); Doubleday Holbeach Depot (1:7, 1:8); Chandlers Ltd (1:5, 2:7); James River Equipment (3:1, 3:9, 2:5); Peter Goddard (3:8). **Dreamstime.com**: Bluetoes67 (2:9, 1:4); Mohammed Anwarul Kabir Choudhury (clb); Jon Helgason (3:2). **Fotolia**: Olena Pantiukh (1:1, 3:4). **Getty Images**: Bloomberg (1:2). J.C. Bamford Excavators Ltd: (3:7). **New Holland Agriculture**: (cla, 3:5). **70 Alamy Stock Photo**: Andia (9:4, 13:2); FLPA (6:7, 9:1, 11:8); John Gaffen 2 (5:6, 8:4, 13:8); William Arthur (3:5); Arco Images GmbH (4:7, 8:2); bronstein (6:3, 12:7). **Dorling Kindersley**: Mick Browning, Tanks, Trucks and Firepower Show (5:4, 12:9); J Hardstaff (3:9); Paul Rackham (4:3, 8:6, 10:1, 2:5, 12:6, 6:2, 10:6, 7:9, 2:4, 9:7, 3:8, 11:4, 3:2, 6:8, 9:3, 2:8, 9:6, 3:1); Lister Wilder (4:2, 6:9); Keystone Tractor Works (5:5, 13:5); Robin Simons (2:3); Roger and Fran Desborough (2:6); Doubleday Holbeach Depot (1:7, 1:8); Chandlers Ltd (1:5, 8:1, 10:9, 8:9, 10:3, 13:4); Henry Flashman (2:7, 11:1); James River Equipment (9:9, 3:6, 7:4, 12:2, 5:9, 7:2, 11:7); Peter Goddard (7:6, 12:1). **Dreamstime.com**: 1000words (3:3); Saša Prudkov (5:1, 10:7); Bluetoes67 (5:8, 10:5, 1:4, 3:7); Mohammed Anwarul Kabir Choudhury (2:1); Jon Helgason (10:2); Alexander Levchenko (10:4, 7:7). **Fotolia**: Olena Pantiukh (1:1, 4:6). **Getty Images**: Bloomberg (1:2); Science & Society Picture Library (2:2). J.C. Bamford Excavators Ltd: (13:9, 6:5, 4:4, 7:1). **New Holland Agriculture**: (5:3, 9:5, 4:5, 11:3). **71 Alamy Stock Photo**: Arco Images GmbH (1:1, 7:7); FLPA (1:8, 7:5, 12:8, 4:5); John Gaffen 2 (7:2, 7:8, 1:6); William Arthur (7:4, 10:5); bronstein (3:4). **Dorling Kindersley**: Mick Browning, Tanks, Trucks and Firepower Show (4:9, 9:1); J Hardstaff (10:9); Paul Rackham (12:1, 1:3, 7:6, 2:3, 5:3, 5:8, 1:9, 6:4, 10:8, 10:2, 12:4, 6:8, 10:1); Lister Wilder (12:3); James River Equipment (13:1, 9:9, 4:2, 5:9, 3:8, 5:1, 8:7, 7:9, 10:6, 3:7, 9:4, 13:9, 5:5, 12:5, 2:7); Keystone Tractor Works (2:5); Robin Simons (6:3); Roger and Fran Desborough (6:6); Doubleday Holbeach Depot (8:6, 11:7, 11:8); Chandlers Ltd (2:1, 11:5, 2:8, 8:4, 12:7); Henry Flashman (6:7); Peter Goddard (13:8, 8:2, 3:5). **Dreamstime.com**: 1000words (10:3); Saša Prudkov (3:3); Bluetoes67 (1:5, 12:9, 1:2, 10:7, 11:4); Mohammed Anwarul Kabir Choudhury (6:1); Jon Helgason (13:2, 9:6, 3:1); Alexander Levchenko (9:7). **Fotolia**: Olena Pantiukh (11:1, 4:1). **Getty Images**: Bloomberg (11:2); Science & Society Picture Library (6:2). **iStockphoto.com**: vbacarin (4:6, 8:9). J.C. Bamford Excavators Ltd: (13:7, 5:4). John Deere Walldorf GmbH & Co. KG: (5:6, 8:8). **New Holland Agriculture**: (5:2, 13:5, 4:8, 2:4, 9:8).

Cover images: *Front*: **123RF.com**: vladimir salman; **Fendt International - AGCO GmbH**: c; **Dorling Kindersley**: James River Equipment bl, Paul Rackham cra; **J.C. Bamford Excavators Ltd**: br; **New Holland Agriculture**: ca, clb; *Back*: **123RF.com**: vladimir salman; **Dorling Kindersley**: Chandlers Ltd tc, J Hardstaff cla, Paul Rackham clb, cb; **New Holland Agriculture**: cra; Versatile: crb

All other images © Dorling Kindersley
For further information see: www.dkimages.com

Contents

What is a tractor?	4–5	On the farm	20–21
Early tractors	6–7	The farming year	22–23
Waterloo Boy	8	Fruit machines	24–25
Cletrac General	9	Monster tractors	26–27
Changing shape	10	Construction tractors	28–29
McCormick International B414	11	Town tractors	30–31
		Specialty tractors	32–33
Modern tractors	12–13	Scene: Plowing and sowing	34–35
Fendt 939 Vario	14		
JCB Fastrac 4220	15	Scene: Building site	36–37
Crawlers	16	Scene: Harvesting	38–39
Challenger MT765D	17	Tractor shows	40
Tractor tires	18–19	Sticker fun!	42–71

What is a tractor?

Tractors are powerful vehicles that are used mainly on farms and building sites. They are slower than cars, but much stronger. Tractors can be equipped with a range of tools, and they can tow heavy loads.

Exhaust
Waste gases from the engine blast out through the exhaust.

Grille
Air can flow in through this mesh to cool the engine.

MASSEY FERGUSON
7618

Weight
Weights attached to the front keep the tractor from tipping back if there's a heavy machine or tool at the rear.

Warning lamp
This light warns people that there is a tractor at work.

DID YOU KNOW?
A tractor engine's power is measured in horsepower (hp). The higher the horsepower, the stronger the tractor.

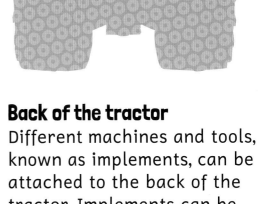

Cab
This compartment keeps the driver safe and comfortable in all types of weather.

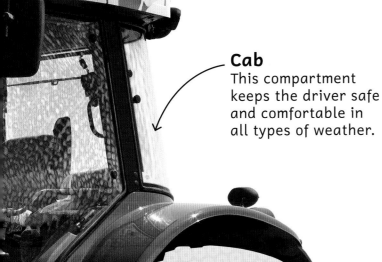

Back of the tractor
Different machines and tools, known as implements, can be attached to the back of the tractor. Implements can be lifted, lowered, and towed.

Inside the cab
All the controls that the driver needs are within reach. There is even room for two people in this cab.

Huge rear wheels
Wheels equipped with chunky tires help the tractor grip well.

Early tractors

The first tractors were made more than 100 years ago. Many companies built these early tractors. They all hoped to make the perfect tractor to sell to as many farmers as possible.

Ivel Agricultural Motor (1902)
British inventor Daniel Albone designed this tractor. It won many awards, but only 500 of them were ever made.

Twin City 40–65 (1916)
This huge tractor was perfect for plowing up the North American prairies. However, it was too big and expensive for most farmers.

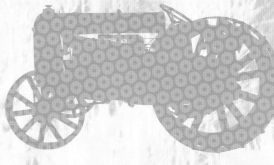

Fordson Model F (1917)
The Model F was lightweight, easy to drive, and cheap. It sold in great numbers and was very popular.

Hart-Parr 18-36 (1927)
This tractor set a world's record by plowing for 11 days. This record helped boost its sales.

Farmall F-20 (1932)
Perfect for working in crop fields, this tractor had narrow wheels that could pass between the rows of plants without causing damage.

John Deere B (1935)
The two front wheels of this popular model were placed very close together. This made the tractor quick and easy to steer and maneuver.

Minneapolis-Moline UDLX (1938)
This unusual-looking tractor was built with a safety cab. No other tractors had cabs at the time.

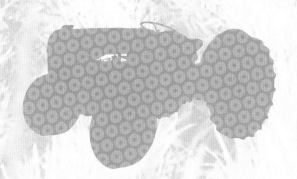

Ford 9N (1939)
This American tractor was the first to have a linkage system in the back for attaching farm implements, such as plows.

Before tractors
Horses used to do the work now done by tractors on farms. They pulled plows and hauled, or dragged, heavy loads.

Waterloo Boy

This tractor is the ancestor of all the green-and-yellow John Deere tractors that you might have seen. The Waterloo Boy is now a rare and very collectible tractor.

FACT FILE

Country: United States
Year first made: 1917
Weight: 6,182 lb (2,804 kg)
Power: 12–25 hp

Side view of Waterloo Boy

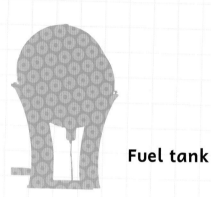

Fuel tank

A radiator on the side of the tractor kept it from overheating.

Kerosene-powered Waterloo Boy

This tractor used the fuel kerosene. It was stored in a tank at the front.

KEROSENE

WATERLOO BOY

The earliest tractors had steel wheels without any rubber tires.

Cletrac General

Three-wheeled, or tricycle, tractors were very popular in the United States in the 1940s. They could be driven along rows of crops without causing damage to the plants.

FACT FILE

Country: United States
Year first made: 1939
Weight: 3,110 lb (1,410 kg)
Power: 17 hp

Side view of Cletrac General

Rear wheel

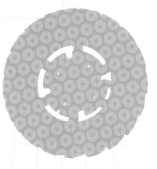

The steering wheel easily turned the single front wheel.

The engine was started by turning a handle in the front.

Tricycle tractor

The body of the tractor was high, so it could drive over crops without damaging them.

Deep treads on rear-wheel tires helped grip soft ground.

Changing shape

By the 1950s, tractors looked a lot like the modern ones on farms today. They were easy to use, and all of them had wheels equipped with rubber tires.

Ferguson TE-20 (1946)
Designed by Irish inventor Harry Ferguson, the TE-20 became one of the world's best-selling tractors. It was nicknamed the "Little Gray Fergie."

Fordson County Super Major 4 (1961)
The English company County took a Fordson tractor and turned it into this much stronger machine with four equal-sized wheels.

Massey Ferguson 35X (1962)
This tractor was a more modern version of the TE-20, above. Extremely well built, it is still popular today.

John Deere 4020 (1964)
With a large, powerful engine and many modern features, the 4020 is still a great favorite with American farmers.

McCormick International B414

Tractors such as the B414 were some of the first to be equipped with cabs to protect the drivers from bad weather. The cab also kept the driver from being hurt if the tractor rolled over.

FACT FILE

Country: Britain
Year first made: 1961
Weight: 3,600–4,050 lb (1,633–1,837 kg)
Power: 44 hp

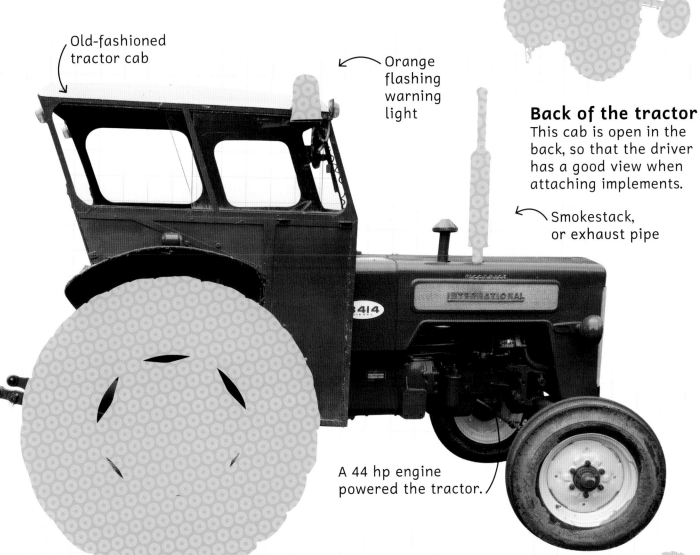

Old-fashioned tractor cab

Orange flashing warning light

Back of the tractor
This cab is open in the back, so that the driver has a good view when attaching implements.

Smokestack, or exhaust pipe

A 44 hp engine powered the tractor.

Modern tractors

Today's amazing tractors come in all shapes and sizes. They have powerful engines that use diesel as fuel. Diesel costs less than other fuels, such as gasoline, and it's easier to use.

Methane tractor

Using diesel as fuel is expensive and can harm the planet. This tractor, made by New Holland, is powered by methane— a natural gas collected from animal manure.

Massey Ferguson 7618

Massey Ferguson began making its famous red tractors in 1958. The 7618 model is many times more powerful than its first tractor.

Zetor Major 80

Built in the Czech Republic, this cheap-to-run tractor has a 76 hp engine. It is ideal for small farms.

John Deere 6215R

The cab of this John Deere tractor is designed for comfort and to give the driver a good view in all directions.

Claas Xerion 3800

The cab sits in between the front and rear wheels, rather than over the back wheels, of this powerful German tractor.

Case IH Puma 230 CVX

Case IH first launched its Puma range of tractors in 2006. The 230 CVX is a useful all-around model with a 231 hp engine.

DID YOU KNOW?
Modern tractors can be equipped with radios, heaters, air conditioning, computer systems, and satellite navigation.

Kubota L3200

This handy little Japanese tractor weighs just 2,425 lb (1,100 kg). It is ideal for working in gardens and orchards.

Fendt 939 Vario

In 1938, the German company Fendt began making small, lightweight tractors. Today, its farm tractors, such as the 939 Vario, are among the largest and most powerful in the world.

FACT FILE

Country: Germany
Year first made: 2010
Weight: 22,840 lb (10,360 kg)
Power: 396 hp

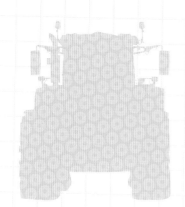

Front view of Fendt 939 Vario

Three-quarter view of Fendt 939 Vario

Mulcher
This implement chops up unwanted plants and clears overgrown land.

Front weights
Weights in the front keep the tractor from tipping back.

JCB Fastrac 4220

JCB is famous for making backhoes and loaders. However, they also make the Fastrac—a high-powered farm tractor that can travel quickly and comfortably on roads.

Wheel of JCB Fastrac 4220

Three-quarter view of JCB Fastrac 4220

Plow
The plow turns over the soil and prepares the field for sowing seeds.

Spacious cab
A Fastrac's cab gives the driver a smooth, comfortable ride, even on bumpy ground.

Powerful engine
Some JCB Fastracs can reach speeds of up to 50 mph (80 kph) on the road.

15

Crawlers

Crawlers are super-strong tractors that move along on steel or rubber tracks instead of wheels. They are perfect for working on steep, bumpy ground or in mud or snow.

John Deere 333E
Ideal on asphalt or concrete surfaces, this loader has rubber tracks that won't cause damage.

Caterpillar D7
This early crawler was a tough machine. It could pull a large plow over steep ground and also work as a bulldozer.

John Deere 160D LC
Used in road building, this backhoe can swivel all the way around while its tracks remain in place.

Fowler Gyrotiller
The special tool at the back of this vintage crawler was used to loosen hard soil.

Challenger MT765D

This powerful farm tractor runs on tracks, which give it a better grip when working on soggy ground. It can haul huge plows through muddy fields without slipping or getting stuck.

FACT FILE

Country: United States
Year first made: 2012
Weight: 31,075 lb (14,095 kg)
Power: 350 hp

Rubber tracks
Unlike steel tracks, rubber tracks do not tear up the ground. They are safe to use on roads.

Wide-tracked crawler
The Challenger's wide tracks spread out its weight. This helps prevent it from sinking into muddy ground.

Side view of Challenger MT765D
The Challenger was the world's first-ever rubber-tracked farm tractor.

FACT!

Tires often get punctured and ripped, but tracks do not. They are super tough!

Weights can be added to balance the tractor.

Tractor tires

Most tractor wheels are equipped with tough rubber tires. The size of the wheel and the tire tread, or pattern, depends on the surfaces the tractor will go on, such as flat parks or muddy fields.

INDUSTRIAL TREAD

Industrial tractors, used mainly on concrete and asphalt roads, have wheels with smaller treads than those on farm tractors. This lets them travel faster over smoother surfaces.

AGRICULTURAL TREAD

The most common tread pattern is found on farm tractors with large tires, such as this John Deere 6210R. The deep, V-shaped grooves help the tractor grip the soft, muddy ground.

Ribbed front tires
The Lanz Bulldog D2206 has front wheels with a ribbed, or lined, pattern. This pattern makes the tires strong and firm.

TURF TREAD

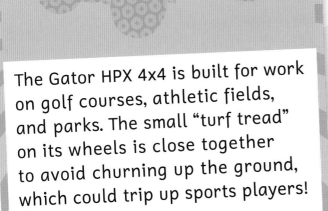

The Gator HPX 4x4 is built for work on golf courses, athletic fields, and parks. The small "turf tread" on its wheels is close together to avoid churning up the ground, which could trip up sports players!

SPADE LUGS

Before rubber tires were used, tractors had steel wheels, as on this Allis Chalmers B from 1939. Pointed "teeth" called spade lugs were attached to the wheels to give them a better grip on muddy soil.

FLOTATION TIRES

Super-wide flotation tires spread the weight of a tractor and keep it from sinking into muddy ground. This huge John Deere 9400 has two sets of wheels with flotation tires to spread the weight even more.

On the farm

Many other machines work alongside tractors on the farm. Implements such as plows can be attached to the back of a tractor. Farms also use "self-propelled" machines, such as combine harvesters, which have their own engines.

Forage harvester

This machine—a Claas Jaguar 860—cuts grass and shoots it through a pipe into a trailer. The cut grass is used to make food for cattle.

Dump trailer

Farmers use trailers to transport heavy loads. This trailer has two sets of wheels to give it extra strength. It can lift at the front and dump its load out of the back.

FACT!

Today's farm workers have to learn how to drive and look after many different machines on the farm.

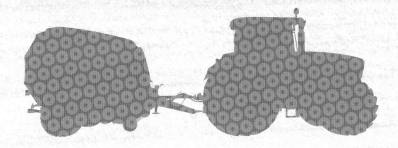

Baler
This John Deere baler makes round bales of hay (mown grass) or straw (dried stalks of cereal plants). The bales are used for animal food and bedding.

Telehandler
The Cat TH406 telehandler can lift, carry, and reach up to 20 ft (6 m) high. It is perfect for stacking hay bales.

Plow
The plow turns over soil, making it ready for sowing seeds. This plow is reversible. It can swivel around and plow the other way.

Combine harvester
The combine harvester, such as this John Deere S690i, is the most important machine on a grain farm. It cuts the crop and separates the grain from the straw.

Manure spreader
Manure, or poop, from farm animals makes good fertilizer for nourishing the soil. This spreader flings manure onto the fields as the tractor drives along.

1. PREPARING SOIL

The plow cuts into the earth and turns it over, laying it upside down in rows called furrows. An implement called a harrow then chops up the soil and loosens it, readying it for planting.

2. SOWING SEEDS

The seed drill is used to add exactly the right amount of seeds to the freshly prepared soil. Some seed drills add fertilizer at the same time that they sow seeds.

The farming year

Tractors keep busy with different jobs throughout the farming year. Farmers work with the weather and seasons, planting crops at the right time to get the best harvest.

3. SPRAYING CROPS

Growing crops can be protected from weeds, pests, and disease by spraying them with chemicals called pesticides. The sprayer has extra-wide arms that let it spray over a large area.

4. HARVESTING CROPS

Once crops have finished growing and are ripe, they are ready for harvesting. The combine harvester does more than one job—it cuts the crop and separates the grain from the straw.

Collecting the grain

Grain in the storage tank of a combine harvester is unloaded through a pipe into a trailer.

Fruit machines

Some tractors are specially built for working on fruit farms. Fruit pickers are often narrow to fit between rows of fruit trees and vines. They can pick fruit without causing any damage to the plants.

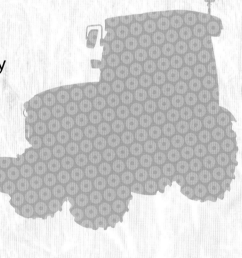

FACT!

Italy is one of the biggest manufacturers of fruit-picking tractors because much of its farmland is vineyards and orchards.

Apple picker
The New Holland T4 can pass below trees to pick fruit, such as apples and nuts. The bars on the front of the tractor protect it from being damaged by branches.

Between the vines
The Fendt 211V is short and very narrow, so that it can squeeze between rows of grapevines in vineyards. Fendt also makes wider models of this tractor.

Grape harvester
The New Holland Braud 9080N is specially designed for picking grapes. It has large mirrors, which allow the driver to see all the way around the machine.

24

Pumpkin harvester

This specially built tractor is used only on pumpkin farms. Workers place pumpkins on a moving belt, which then takes them into a tank to be cleaned.

Straddle tractor

The Tecnoma T140 can pass over, or straddle, tall crops to avoid damaging them. Here, it is spraying vines with pesticides.

Olive picker

Olive pickers such as this New Holland Braud 9090X have built-in storage tanks called hoppers. This is where the olives are collected once they are removed from the trees.

Hill climber

Crawlers are more stable than wheeled tractors on steep hills. This Massey-Ferguson 3350C is ideal for moving around sloping vineyards and olive groves.

Monster tractors

These heavyweight machines have the strength to pull extra-wide plows and huge implements over rough or muddy ground. They are the giants of the tractor world!

Challenger MT965C
This huge 570 hp tractor comes with wheels or tracks. Wheels are suited to roadwork, but tracks are better for muddy fields.

Kirovets K-700A
Built in Russia, Kirovets tractors are strong and powerful. However, some drivers find them very noisy, so ear protection is really important!

New Holland T9.505
Steps help the driver climb up to the high cab. For a better grip, this tractor can be equipped with double wheels.

Versatile Big Roy
Only one Versatile Big Roy was ever made. Built in 1977, this monster with an eight-wheel drive now lives in a museum in Canada.

Fendt Trisix

German company Fendt built this six-wheel-drive concept, or experimental, tractor. It never went into full production but gave rise to the Fendt 1000 series.

Case IH Steiger® Quadtrac® 620

Some massive tractors are equipped with triangular tracks instead of wheels. These tracks provide a better grip in wet, muddy soil.

John Deere 9RX

Large tractors can be clumsy, but this tracked tractor can bend in the middle. That makes it easier to steer around corners.

FACT!

Giant tractors can damage the ground. Spreading out the tractor's weight with wide wheels or tracks helps prevent damage.

Construction tractors

All kinds of specialized tractors and machines work on our roads and building sites. Most construction-site vehicles are yellow, so that people can easily see them.

Articulated dump truck
Dump trucks come in all sizes. This giant Caterpillar 725 is articulated, which means it can bend in the middle.

Bulldozer
This John Deere 650K XLT is perfect for working on rough ground. The huge front blade can flatten piles of soil, sand, or stone.

Scraper

This Caterpillar 615C cuts into the ground and scrapes away the top layer of soil. It makes the ground level as it moves along.

Backhoe

An all-purpose machine on a construction site, this JCB 3CX backhoe can dig, lift, and load with its two different-sized buckets.

Roller

This Sakai SV400 roller moves slowly and is super heavy. It has a "sheepsfoot" roller drum with large pegs that crush and pack down surfaces.

Front loader

Working like a giant scoop, this Case 621B can shovel and carry huge loads of stone or sand.

Boom crawler

Laying pipes is the job of this Caterpillar 583T boom crawler. The pipes are lowered into place using its tall crane.

Town tractors

Many different kinds of tractors can be seen at work in towns and cities. They keep our roads, grass, parks, and athletic fields in good condition.

DID YOU KNOW?
Tractors used for working on athletic fields usually have smooth tires that won't mark the grass.

Massey Ferguson 6455
The mowing implement on the back of this tractor is used to cut roadside grass, embankments, and hedges.

John Deere 3045R
This little tractor is often seen in parks. It can be equipped with a cab and a front loader for moving soil or gravel.

Unimog U400

Powerful and adaptable, the Unimog can do many jobs, including sweeping and snow plowing. It can even travel on railroad tracks.

John Deere Z445

Instead of using a steering wheel, you turn this mower with levers. It is super fast and very easy to handle.

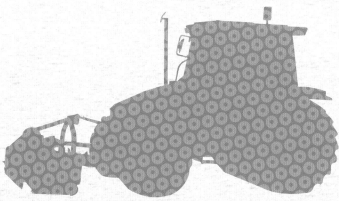

Massey Ferguson 3065

This tractor has a mower attached to the front. The mower can be lifted and lowered and is perfect for cutting large areas of grass.

FACT!

Tractors can be dangerous machines. The flashing lights on town tractors warn people to keep clear.

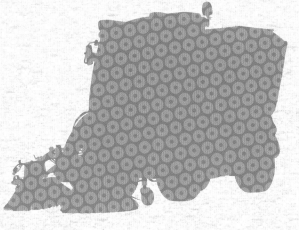

Schmidt AS 990

This machine is set up as a street sweeper. However, it can also be a snowplow, mower, or mobile water tank!

Specialty tractors

These unusual-looking machines are specialty tractors. They are cleverly designed to do different, important, and sometimes lifesaving work in many parts of the world.

John Deere 843K Feller Buncher

This forestry tractor has massive jaws to grab tree trunks and a powerful saw to cut through the timber.

Alvis FV103 Spartan

This bombproof crawler is designed to transport soldiers in war zones. It can handle the roughest ground and travel up to 60 mph (95 kph).

Talus MB-H

Watertight and extremely strong, this crawler is used to haul heavy lifeboats into and out of the sea.

Grimme Rexor 620

Like a factory on wheels, this huge harvester digs up sugar beets, cuts off their leaves, and cleans the big white roots.

PistenBully PB260D

Extra-wide tracks let this crawler glide over snow and ice. Its huge blade can clear and smooth the snow on ski slopes.

TLD TMX Aircraft Tug

This low-to-the-ground heavyweight tug is designed to tow and maneuver enormous airplanes into place at airports.

Plowing and sowing

CHECKLIST

Use the stickers in the book to fill up this scene. You might see the items listed below in the fields when it's time to prepare the land for crops and plant them.

- [ ] Cultivator
- [ ] Fertilizer
- [ ] Land roller
- [ ] Harrow
- [ ] Manure spreader
- [ ] Plow
- [ ] Seed drill

Building site

CHECKLIST

Use the stickers in the book to fill up this scene. You might see the items listed below on a building site.

- Articulated dump truck
- Backhoe
- Boom crawler
- Bulldozer
- Construction worker
- Front loader
- Hard hat
- Roller
- Rubble
- Scraper

Harvesting

CHECKLIST

Use the stickers in the book to fill up the scene. You might see the items listed below in the fields when farmers harvest their cereal crops.

- [ ] Bale grabber
- [ ] Baler
- [ ] Combine harvester
- [ ] Forklift tractor
- [ ] Trailer

Tractor shows

Many tractor owners are proud of their vehicles and like to take them to shows, competitions, and parades. At these events, people can enjoy seeing tractors at work and play.

PULLING CONTEST

Drivers compete to see who has the strongest tractor. Many of these specialty tractors have been equipped with super-powerful engines to give them the extra strength needed to win.

PLOWING COMPETITION

Plowing is an important part of a farmer's job—and it is also an international sport! Old and new tractors compete in different classes to see which ones are the best at plowing.

DANCING DIGGERS

One event that never fails to wow the crowd is the "Dancing Diggers." Highly skilled backhoe drivers perform all kinds of crazy stunts with their tractors' digging buckets and arms.

Back of the MF 7618 tractor

Grille of MF 7618

Exhaust pipe
of MF 7618

Rear wheel of MF 7618

Weight attached to MF 7618

Warning
lamp of
MF 7618

Fordson Model F

Front wheel
of MF 7618

Twin City 40-65

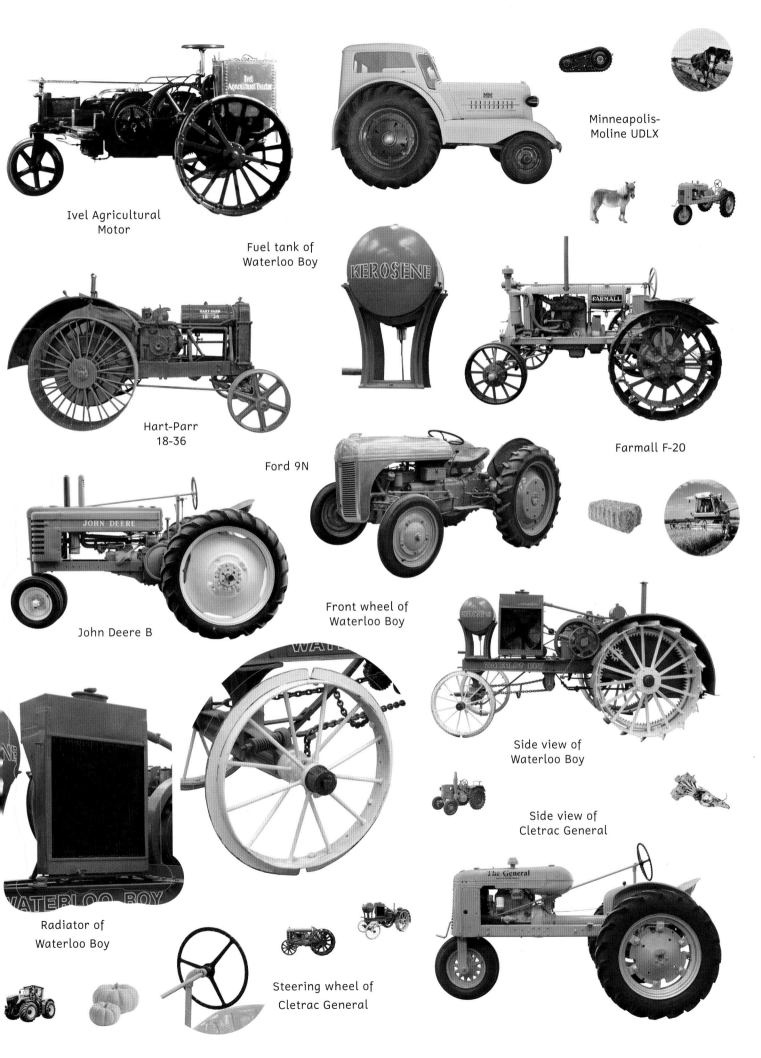

Ivel Agricultural
Motor

Minneapolis-
Moline UDLX

Fuel tank of
Waterloo Boy

KEROSENE

Hart-Parr
18-36

Ford 9N

Farmall F-20

John Deere B

Front wheel of
Waterloo Boy

Side view of
Waterloo Boy

Side view of
Cletrac General

Radiator of
Waterloo Boy

Steering wheel of
Cletrac General

Ferguson
TE-20

Fordson County Super Major 4

Warning
light of B414

John Deere
4020

Massey
Ferguson 35X

Kubota L3200

John Deere
6215R

Massey
Ferguson 7618

Claas
Xerion 3800

Methane
tractor

Case IH Puma
230 CVX

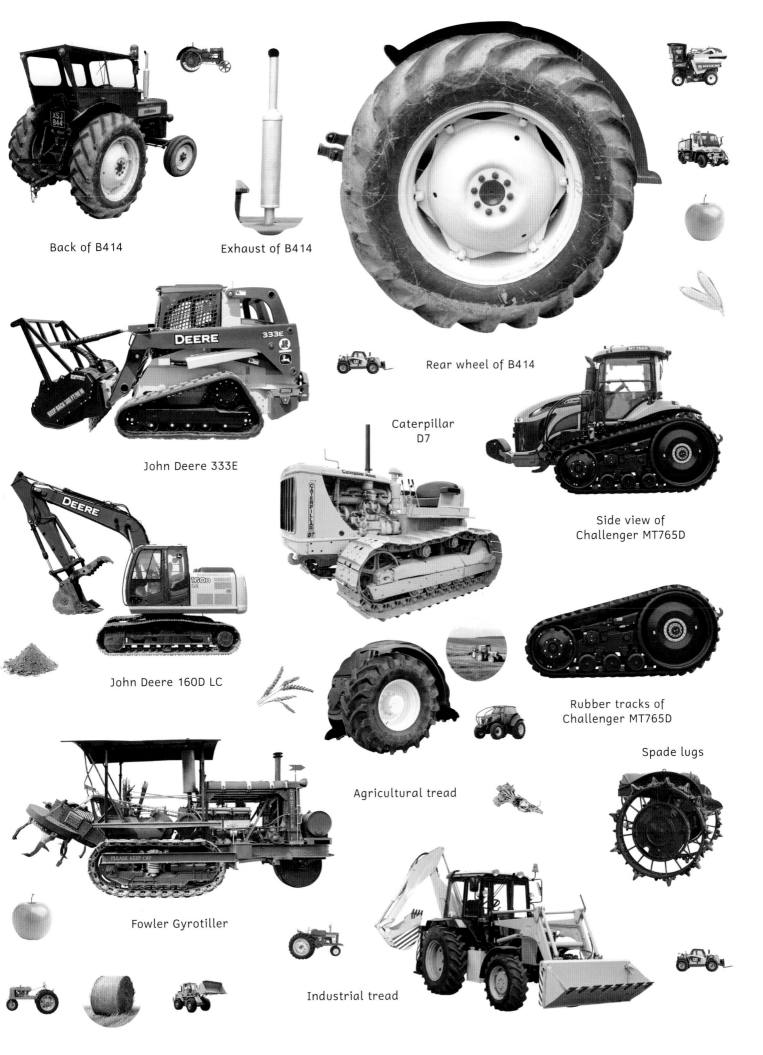

Back of B414

Exhaust of B414

Rear wheel of B414

John Deere 333E

John Deere 160D LC

Caterpillar D7

Side view of Challenger MT765D

Rubber tracks of Challenger MT765D

Agricultural tread

Spade lugs

Fowler Gyrotiller

Industrial tread

Flotation tires

Turf tread

Rear wheel of
Cletrac General

Spraying crops

Front wheel of
Cletrac General

Sowing
seeds

Wheel of JCB
Fastrac 4220

Bulldozer

Front view of Fendt
939 Vario

Three-quarter
view of Fendt
939 Vario

Three-quarter view of
JCB Fastrac 4220

Harvesting
crops

Preparing
soil

Rear wheel of Fendt
939 Vario

Manure spreader

Plow

Combine harvester

Massey Ferguson 6455

Plow of JCB
Fastrac 4220

Forage
harvester

Telehandler

Baler

Dump trailer

Kirovets K-700A

Scraper

Versatile Big Roy

Front loader

Articulated dump truck

Talus MB-H

Roller

Backhoe

Boom crawler

Grimme
Rexor 620

John Deere
3045R

Dancing
diggers

Between
the vines

Fendt Trisix

John Deere 843K
Feller Buncher

Alvis FV103 Spartan

TLD TMX
Aircraft Tug

Grape
harvester

Hill climber

Olive picker

PistenBully PB260D

Tractor in pulling contest

New Holland T9.505

Pumpkin harvester

Tractor in plowing competition

Challenger MT965C

Case IH Steiger
Quadtrac 620

Apple picker

Unimog U400

John
Deere 9RX

Schmidt
AS 990

Massey
Ferguson
3065

John Deere
Z445

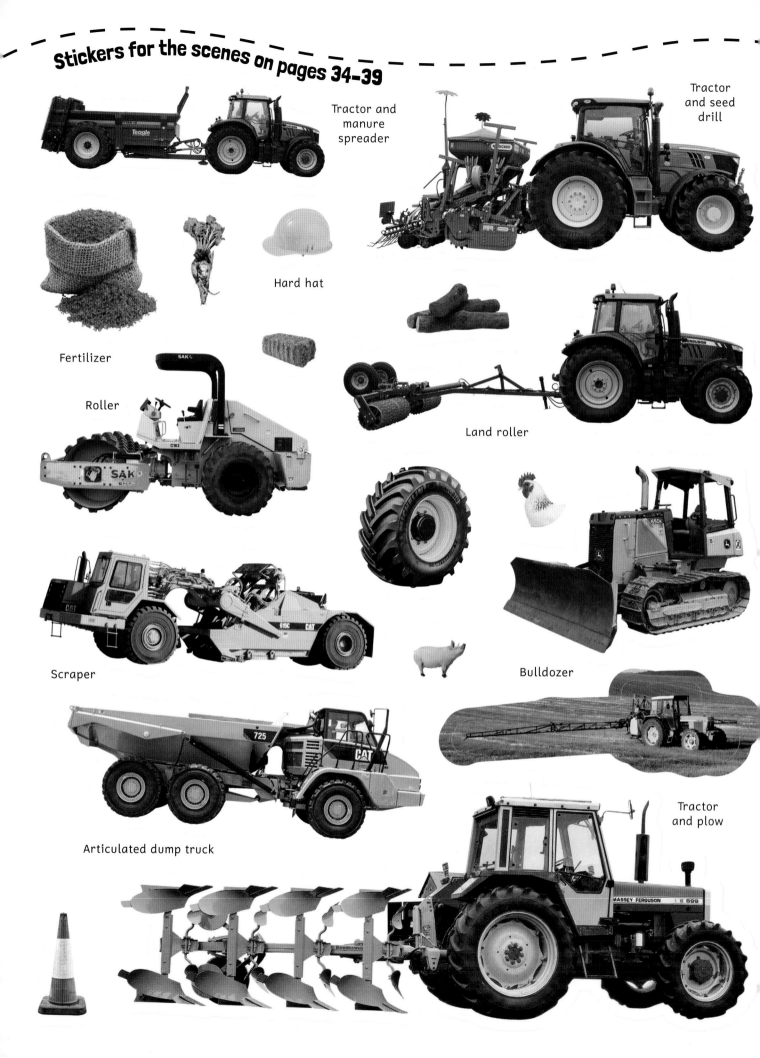

Stickers for the scenes on pages 34-39

Tractor and manure spreader

Tractor and seed drill

Hard hat

Fertilizer

Roller

Land roller

Scraper

Bulldozer

Articulated dump truck

Tractor and plow

Tractor
and baler

Tractor
and
harrow

Bale grabber

Construction worker

Boom
crawler

Backhoe

Combine
harvester

Rubble

Tractor and
cultivator

Front
loader

Trailer

Forklift tractor